How To Draw The Fashion World
Amit Offir

All rights reserved. No part of this book may be translated, reproduced, stored in a retrieval system or transmitted, in any form or by any means, electronic, photocopying, recording or otherwise, without prior permission in writing from the author and publisher.

www.troubadour.co.il

Copyrights © 2013 by Amit Offir

© www.troubadour.co.il

How to draw fashion world

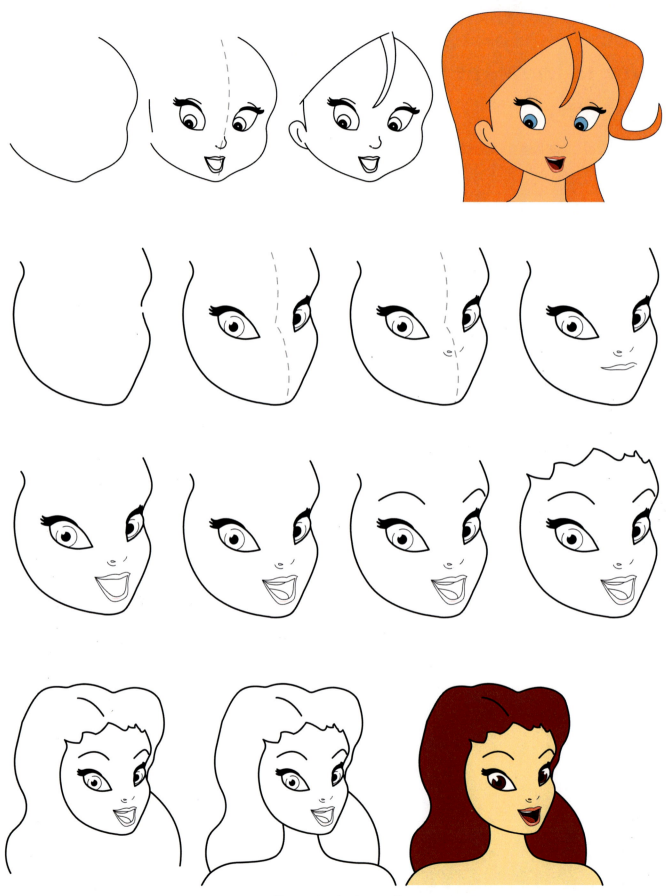

© www.troubadour.co.il

How to draw fashion world

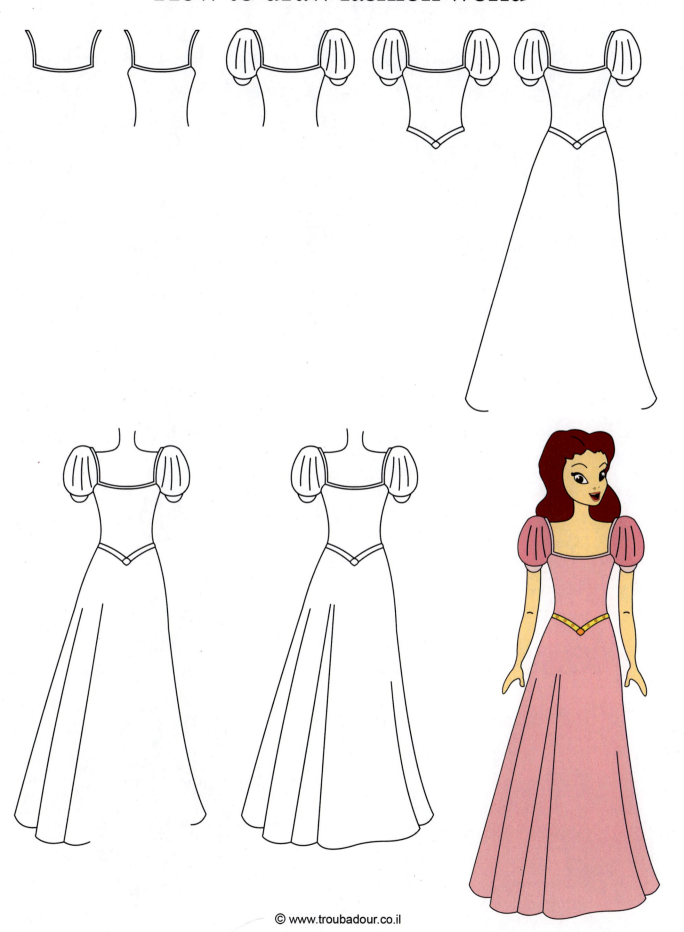

How to draw fashion world

© www.troubadour.co.il

How to draw fashion world

How to draw fashion world

How to draw fashion world

How to draw fashion world

How to draw fashion world

How to draw fashion world

© www.troubadour.co.il

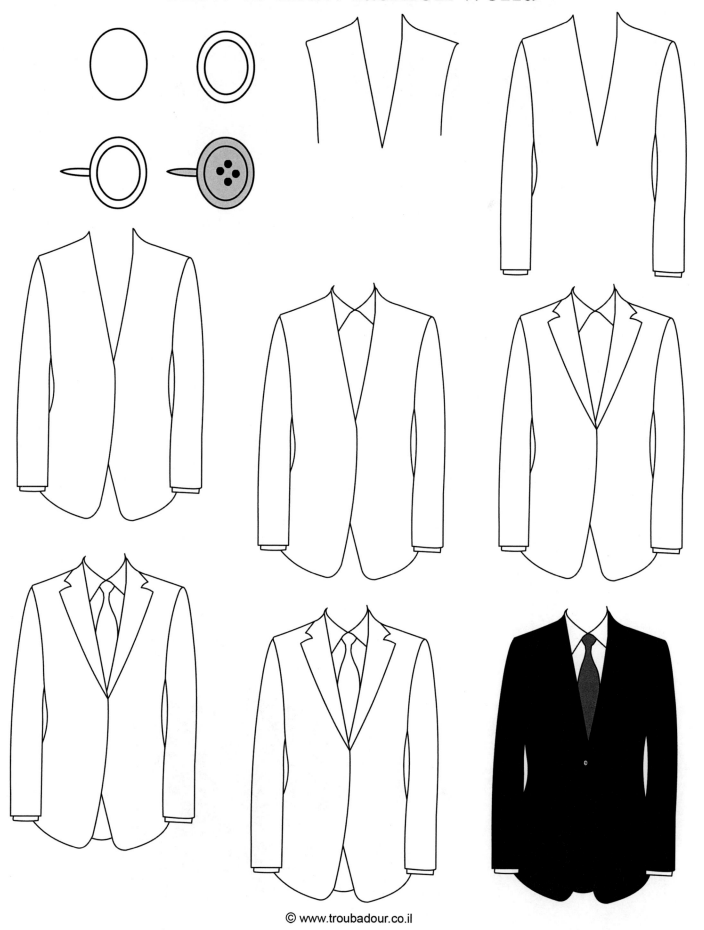

How to draw fashion world

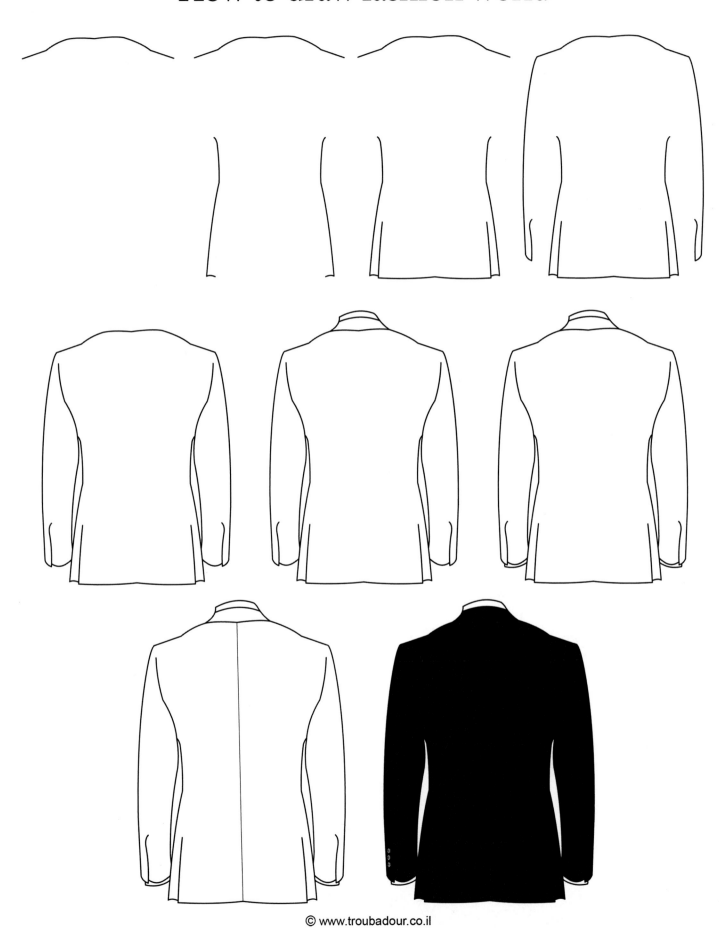

www.troubadour.co.il

How to draw fashion world

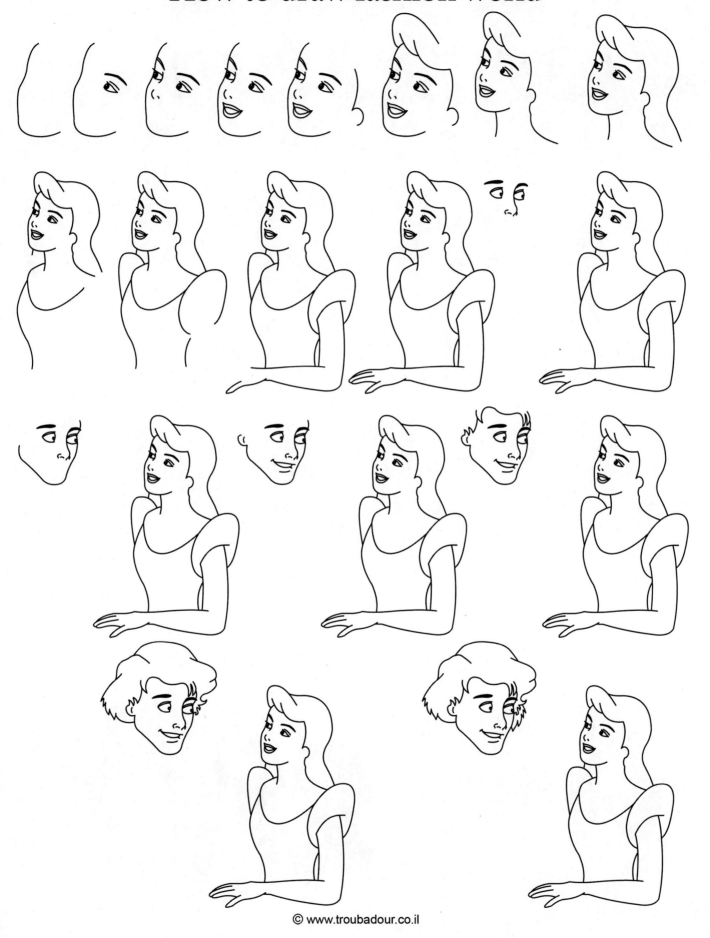

© www.troubadour.co.il

How to draw fashion world

How to draw fashion world

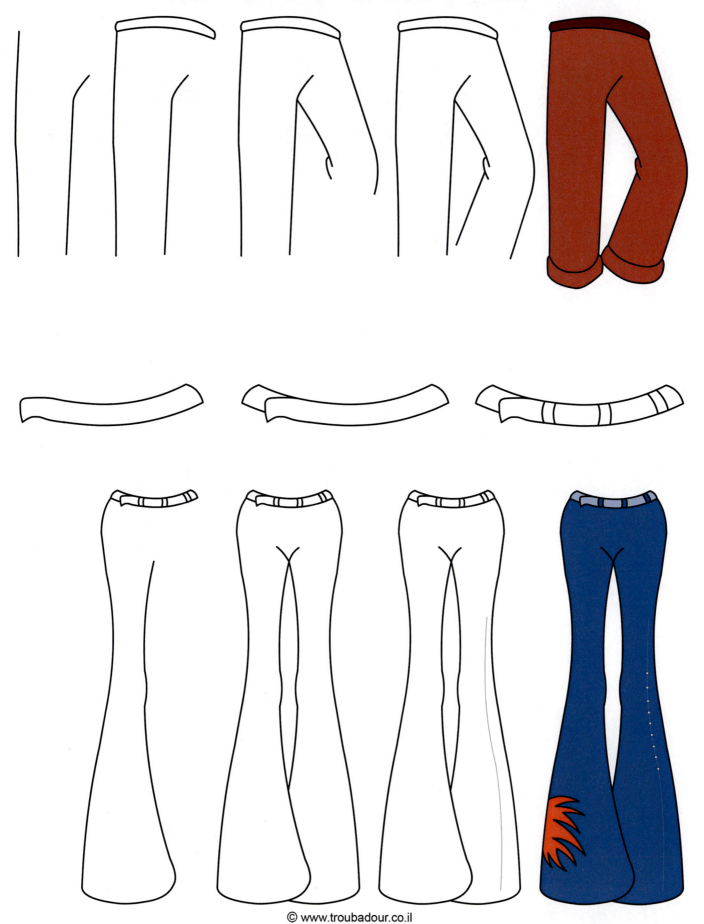

How to draw fashion world

How to draw fashion world

© www.troubadour.co.il

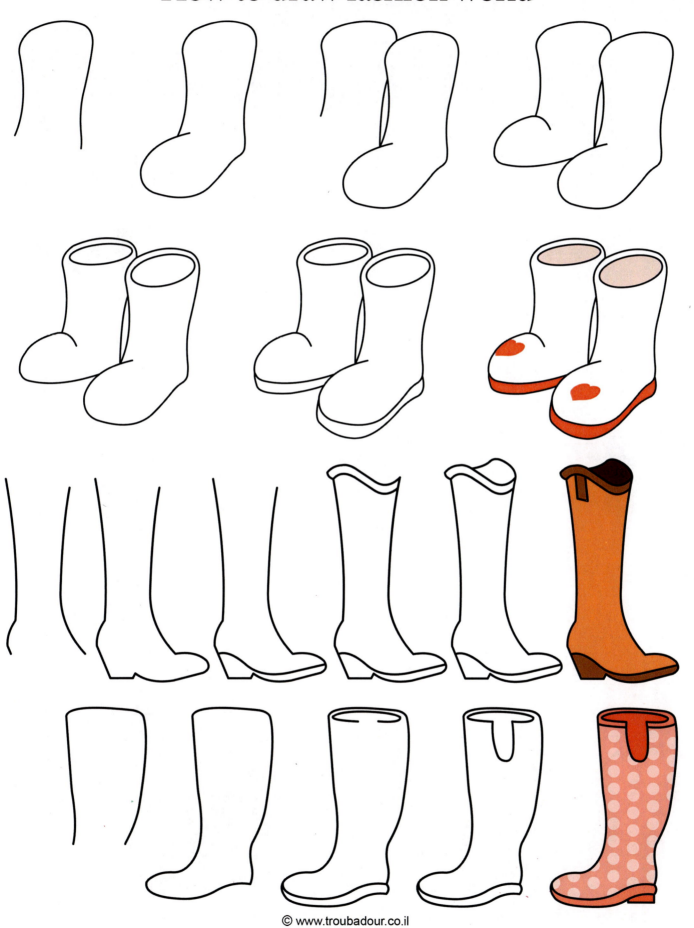

How to draw fashion world

How to draw fashion world

How to draw fashion world

How to draw fashion world

© www.troubadour.co.il

How to draw fashion world

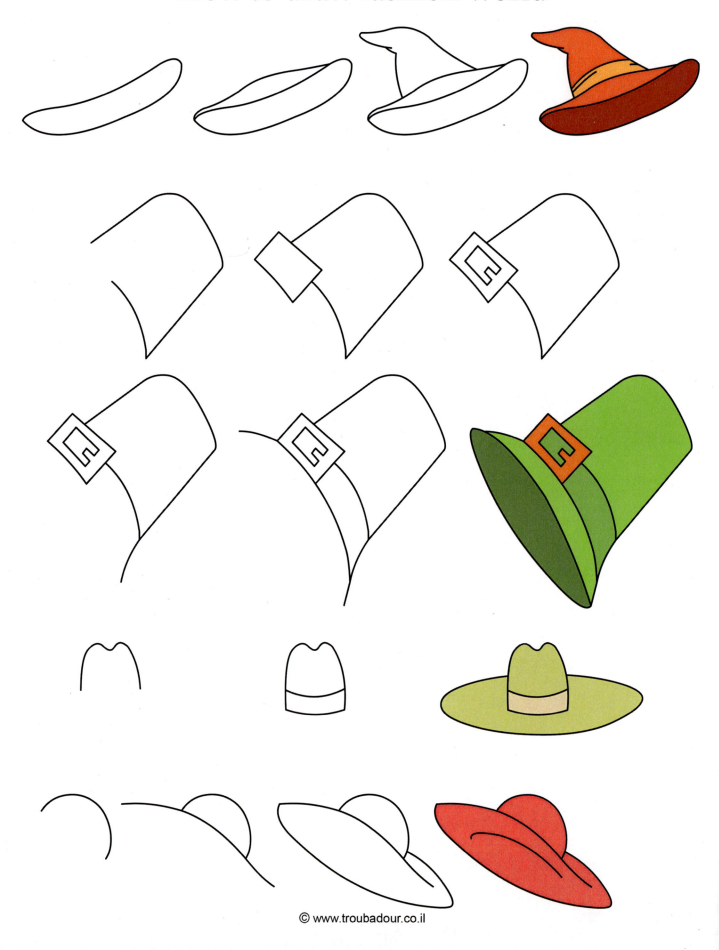

How to draw fashion world

© www.troubadour.co.il

How to draw fashion world

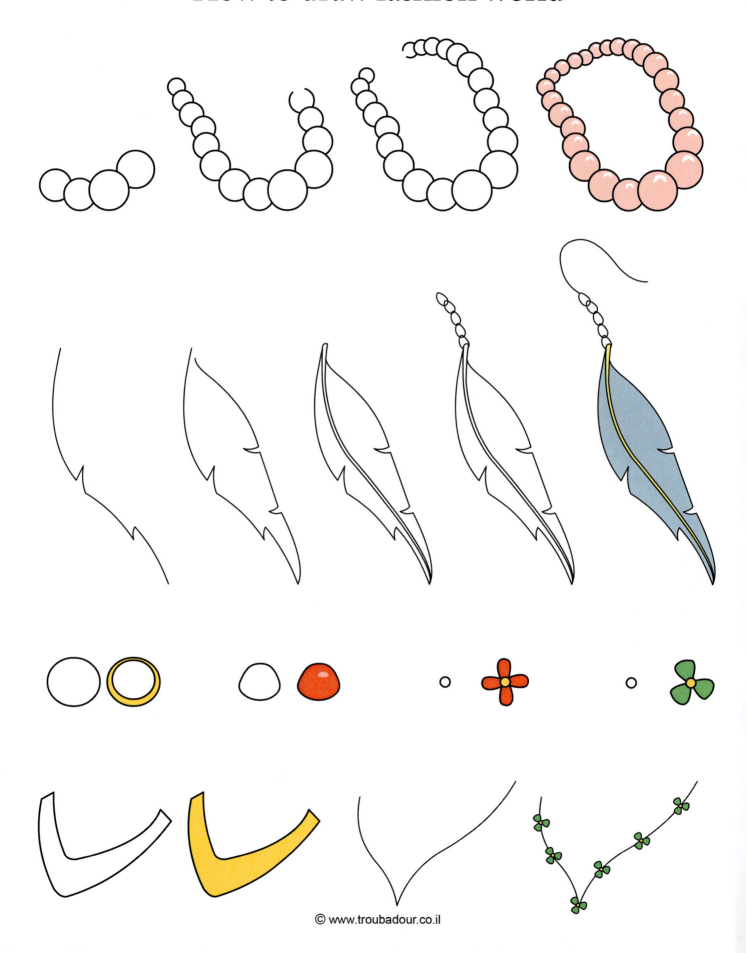

© www.troubadour.co.il

How to draw fashion world

How to draw fashion world

How to draw fashion world

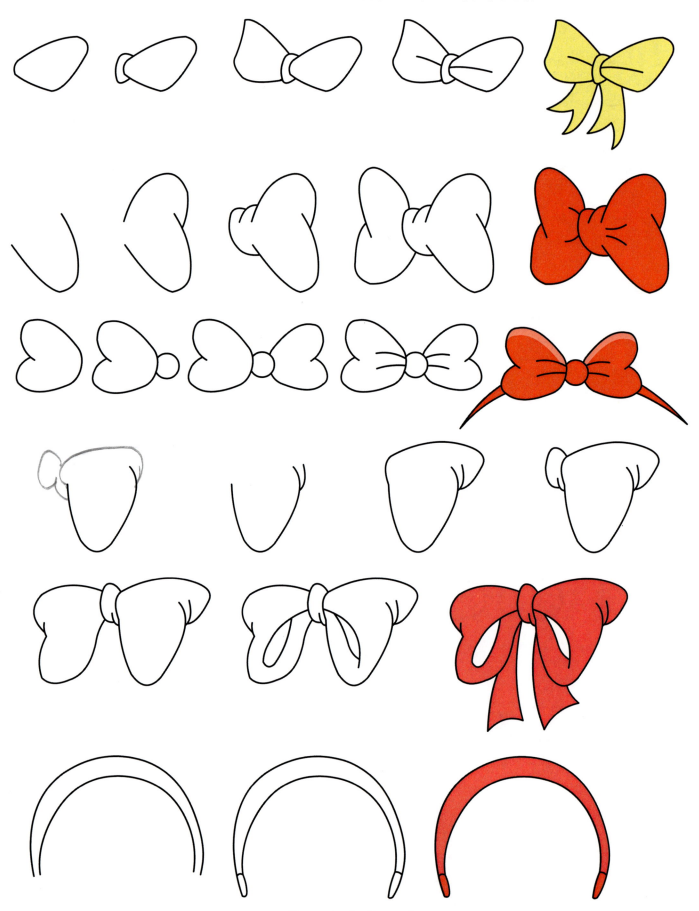

How to draw fashion world

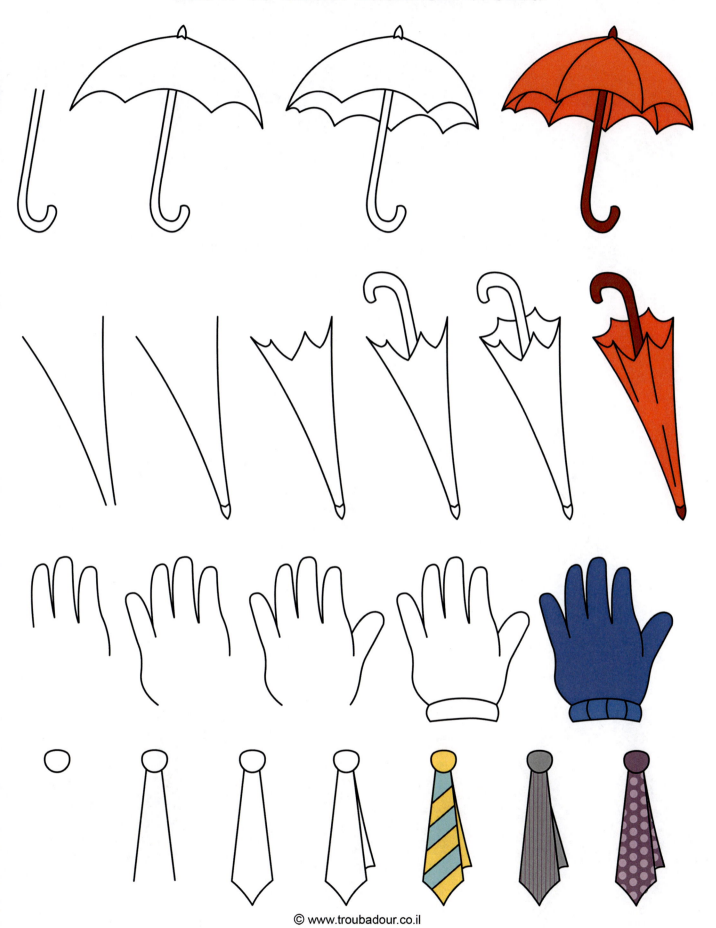

© www.troubadour.co.il

How to draw fashion world

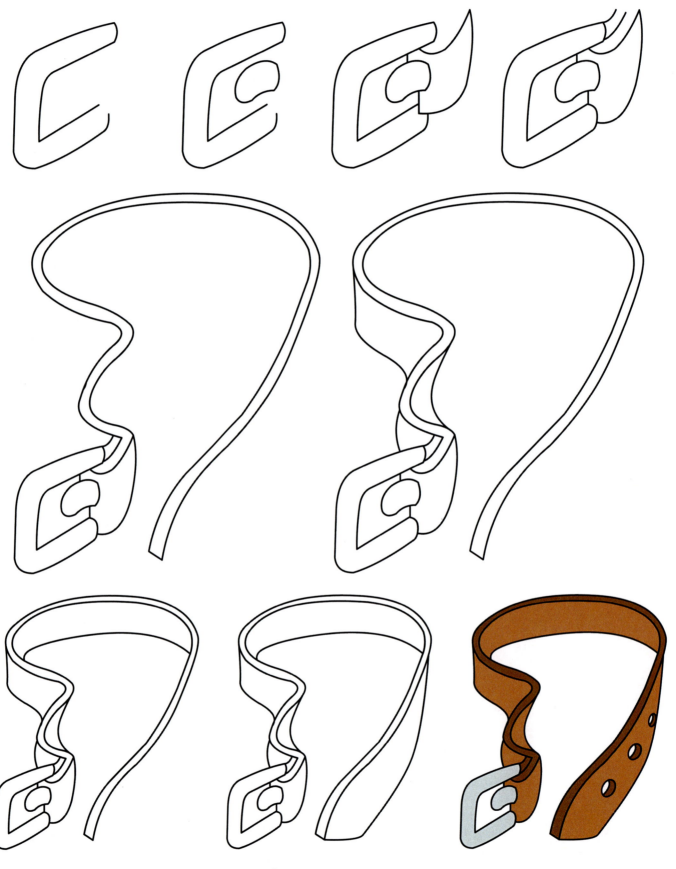

© www.troubadour.co.il

How to draw fashion world

About The Author

Amit Offir is a renowned illustrator, author, and comics artist.

His first book "The Beetle That Wants To Be" is one of his bestsellers.

On the year 2005 he developed a uniqe technique for drawing comics and cartoon characters in a few easy steps.

He named it "Drawing Easily".

This technique was invented after drawing over 500,000 drawings on stones.

Amit lectures and teaches comics lessons and meets thousands of children and adults every year around the world.

You are welcome to get farther information about Amit Offir's art, licensing and more, in the "Troubadour" official website www.troubadour.co.il

Enjoy this series of books and keep on drawing!

Best regards.

© www.troubadour.co.il

Books in this series

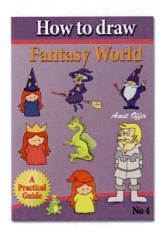 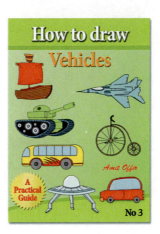 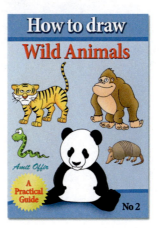 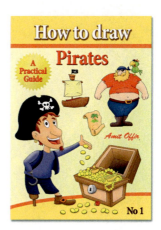

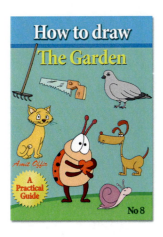 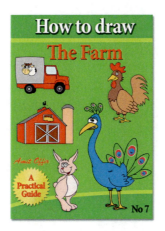 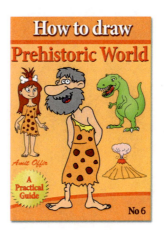 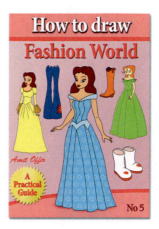

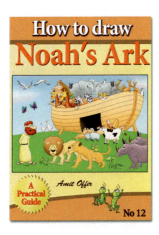 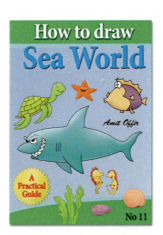 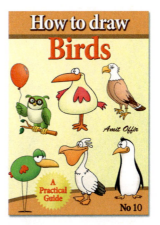 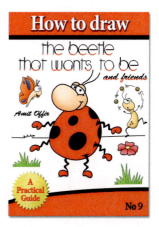

And many more!

Enter the official website - www.troubadour.co.il

Made in the USA
Middletown, DE
12 December 2015